Country Kitchen Collection
Harvest Fare

Isaac Henzell (fl.1854–1875) *The Gleaners*

Country Kitchen Collection
Harvest Fare
Anna Nicholas

William Kay Blacklock (ex.1897–1921) *Mother and Child with Harvesters*

ACKNOWLEDGEMENTS
All pictures by courtesy of The Bridgeman Art Library.

Haytime by Rosa Appleton (fl.1888-1920) Christopher Wood Gallery, London/Bridgeman Art Library, London. One of the Family by Frederick George Cotman (1850-1920) Walker Art Gallery, Liverpool/ Bridgeman Art Library, London. The Saffron Cake by Alexander Stanhope Forbes (1857-1947) Private collection /Bridgeman Art Library, London. Dixton Harvesters, c.1725 (Detail No. 6 of 68500), English School of the 18th century, Cheltenham Art Gallery and Museums, Gloucestershire/Bridgeman Art Library, London. Still Life with Bread by Osias Beert the Elder (1570-1624) Alan Jacobs Gallery, London/Bridgeman Art Library, London. Cherry Ripe by William Frederick Yeames (1835-1918) Hartlepool Museum Service/ Bridgeman Art Library, London. Mother and Child with Harvesters by William Kay Blacklock (fl.1897-1921) John Noott Galleries, Broadway, Worcs./Bridgeman Art Library, London. The Gleaners by Isaac Henzell (fl.1854-75). Atkinson Art Gallery, Southport, Lancs./ Bridgeman Art Library, London. Saying Grace by Arthur Hughes (1832-1915) Maidstone Museum and Art Gallery, Kent/Bridgeman Art Gallery, London. Still Life with a Bottle of Olives by Jean-Baptiste Simeon (1699-1779) Louvre, Paris, Bridgeman Art Library/Giraudon. Preserving Jam by Frederick Daniel Hardy Chardin (1826-1911) Bourne Gallery, Reigate, Surrey/Bridgeman Art Library. Woman Haymaking by Camille Pissarro (1830-1903) Dr. H.C.E. Drefus Foundation, Kunstmuseum, Basle/Bridgeman Art Library, London. The Gleaners by Joshua Cristall (1767-1847) Haworth Art Gallery, Accrington, Lancs./Bridgeman Art Library. Harvesters' Lunch by Peter Brueghel the Younger (c.1564-1638) Christie's, London/Bridgeman Art Library, London. The Winnowers by Gustave Courbet (1819-1877) Musée des Beaux-Arts, Nantes/ Bridgeman Art Library. The Fruit Seller by Jan Victors (1620-1676) Johnny van Haeften Gallery, London/Bridgeman Art Library, London. Snapp Apple Night by Daniel Maclise (1806-1870) Phillips, The International Fine Art Auctioneers/Bridgeman Art Library, London. The Harvester's Supper by Henry Hubert La Thangue (1859-1929) Bradford Art Galleries and Museums/Bridgeman Art Library, London. The Siesta, 1899 by Camille Pissarro (1830-1903) Durand-Ruel Collection, Paris/Bridgeman Art Library, London. Banquet Still Life by Jacob Foppens van Es (c.1596-1666) Alan Jacobs Gallery, London/Bridgeman Art Library, London. Tending the Cabbage Patch by Maud Naftel (1856-1890) Christopher Wood Gallery, London/Bridgeman Art Library. The Bakery by Helene Schjerfbeck (1862-1946) Pohjanmaan Museo, Vaasa/Bridgeman Art Library. Harvesting at Montfoucault, 1876 by Camille Pissarro (1831-1903) Musée d'Orsay, Paris/Bridgeman Art Library, London/Giraudon. A Harvest Feast circle of Frans Francken the Elder (1542-1616) Bonhams, London/Bridgeman Art Library, London. Reciting an Ode on Mamma's Birthday by Angelo Martinetti (19th century) Bonhams, London/Bridgeman Art Library, London. Apple Pickers, Eragny, 1888 by Camille Pissarro (1830-1903) Dallas Museum of Fine Arts, Texas/Bridgeman Art Library, London. The Veteran in a New Field by Winslow Homer (1836-1910) Metropolitan Museum of Art, New York/ Bridgeman Art Library, London. The Harvest by C.H. Hart (19th century) Private Collection/Bridgeman Art Library, London. Preparing the Punch by Walter Dendy Sadler (1854-1923) John Noote Galleries, Broadway, Worcs.,/Bridgeman Art Library, London. The Table by Clara Peeters (1594-1659) Prado, Madrid/Bridgeman Art Library. Gathering Grapes by Daniel Ridgeway (1839-1924) Private Collection/Bridgeman Art Library.

The Publishers have made every effort to trace the copyright holders of material reproduced within this compilation. If, however, they have inadvertantly made any error they would be grateful for notification.

Published in 1996
by Grange Books
An imprint of Grange Books Plc.
The Grange
Grange Yard
London SE1 3AG

ISBN 1 85627 734 8

Copyright © 1996 Regency House Publishing Limited

Printed in China

This book is not intended to be an in-depth look at the technique of cooking: there are a myriad of books which do just this and which go into the nuances of producing many of the dishes described in this volume, most of which have been around for a very long time and exist in many variations even across national boundaries. It is a celebration of food in its wider sense; as an important part of the development of civilized behaviour in which society is bonded together in the acts of eating, discussing and depicting food which is, after all, a prime necessity for our continued existence.

'Season of mists and mellow fruitfulness!
Close bosom-friend of the maturing sun;
Conspiring with him how to load and bless
With fruit the vines that round the
thatch-eaves run;
To bend with apples the moss'd cottage-trees,
And fill all fruit with ripeness to the core;
To swell the gourd, and plump the hazel shells
With a sweet kernel; to set budding more,
And still more, later flowers for the bees.
Until they think warm days will never cease,
For Summer has o'er-brimmed their
clammy cells.'

John Keats (1795-1821) From *To Autumn*

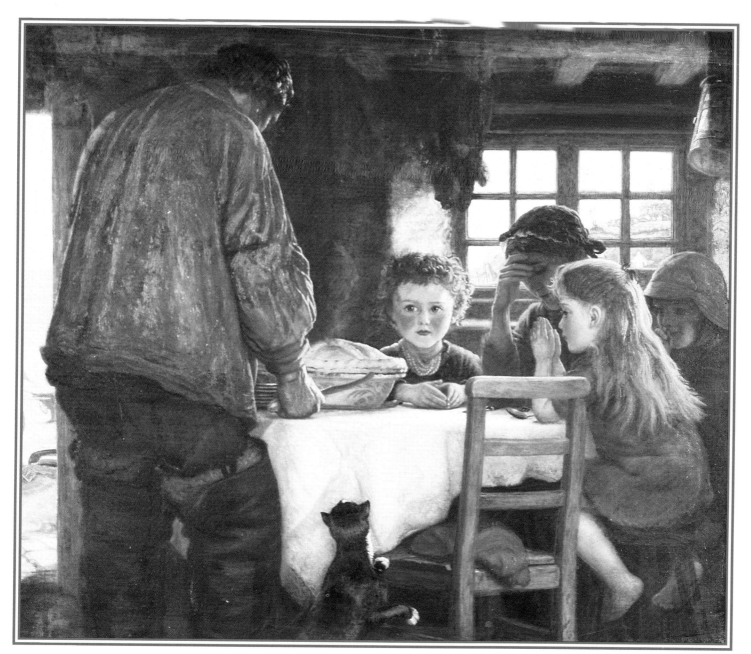

Arthur Hughes (1832–1915) *Saying Grace*

Foreword

Autumn is the time of the year when we suddenly realize that there is a sharp nip in the air and we must regretfully bid farewell to the long, lazy days of summer. But there are compensations. Now come preparations for the harvest festival and we start to look forward to Thanksgiving, blazing fires and, ultimately, the Christmas season.

If we grow our own fruit and vegetables, and an increasing number of us do, we will inevitably find ourselves faced with a glut when we are suddenly confronted with the problem of what to do with the surplus produce.

The age-old answer is to fill the pantry with jams and jellies, preserves and pickles, chutneys and home-made fruit liqueurs. In the past, finding ways of preserving food was of tantamount importance. Deep freezers and refrigerators were once unheard of and country people especially, would have faced a very lean winter indeed without their dried and salted meats, fish and bottled vegetables and preserves.

Today we do not face quite the same problems but these atavistic feelings still persist, emerging from time to time in the form of tremendous feelings of satisfaction when we view our rows of colourful jars and bottles displayed upon the larder shelf and think of the wonderful winter meals we will be able to produce from our precious hoard.

'And fruit and leaf are as gold as fire
And the oat is heard above the lyre.'

Augustus Charles Swinburne (1837-1909) *Atlanta on Calydon*

Jean-Baptiste Chardin (1699-1779) *Still Life with a Bottle of Olives*

Tapénade

A simple black olive paste, useful for spreading on crusty bread and adding to sauces, mayonnaise and pizza can be made in a food processor with 10 oz (2 cups) pitted olives, a small onion (chopped), 3 cloves of garlic, and 2 tablespoons olive oil. Put all the ingredients in the bowl and give them a whizz. The paste will keep for several weeks in the refrigerator, packed in sterilized jars, the contents covered with a thin layer of oil. The more authentic Provençal version would have a little flaked tuna and a few anchovies, capers and lemon juice added to make this a more substantial hors d'oeuvres to be served with hard-boiled eggs.

The sense of taste is the most exquisite of all.
Cicero (106-43 B.C.)

Redcurrant Jelly

This is a somewhat simplified version of Eliza Acton's classic 19th-century recipe. While the same clarity may not be achieved, the wonderful taste and jewel-like colour will still be very much apparent.

For this recipe you will need 2 lb (1 kg) sugar to the same amount of redcurrants which have been stripped from their stalks. Place the fruit in a preserving pan and bring slowly to the boil, pressing the redcurrants to encourage them to release their juice. As soon as the fruit is cooked, add the warmed sugar, stir until dissolved and bring to a rapid boil for 8 minutes. Place in a nylon sieve lined with two layers of gauze and let the fruit mixture drip through, pressing slightly to extract as much juice as possible. Store in sterilized jars covered with waxed paper discs and tied down.

The rule is, jam tomorrow and jam yesterday — but never jam today.

Lewis Carroll (1832-1898)

George Frederick Cotman (1850-1920) *One of the Family*

Seville Orange Marmalade

Be sure to make good use of these special oranges which are available for such a short time. No other kind will do.

Wash and shred 2 lb (1 kg) Seville oranges together with one lemon and leave to soak overnight in 4 pints (2½ quarts) of water. Next day, bring everything to the boil in a large saucepan and simmer gently for 1½ hours or until the peel is soft and the contents of the saucepan have reduced to about half. Add 4 lb (2 kg) sugar, stir until it is all dissolved and boil for a further 15 minutes. Test for setting by dropping a spoonful of the marmalade onto a cold plate. Allow the marmalade to cool a little before putting it into jars.

Frederick Daniel Hardy (1826–1911) *Preserving Jam*

Apple Charlotte

The apple is one of the most universally loved of fruits and is a recurring symbol in religion and mythology.

Cut 1 lb (450 g) peeled cooking apples into ¹/₂-inch dice, put in a saucepan and cook very slowly together with 8 oz (I cup) sugar, 2 oz (4 tablespoons) butter, the rind and juice of half a lemon, 3 tablespoons apricot preserve and a good pinch of ground cinnamon. When soft, add 2 oz (¹/₂ cup) skinned almonds.

Meanwhile, line a buttered pudding basin with overlapping triangles of white bread dipped in melted butter. Do not leave any gaps. Beat 1 egg into the cooled apple mixture, pour into the pudding basin and seal the top with more bread. Leave to rest weighed down with a plate with a heavy ovenproof object on top and bake, still weighted, at 400°F (200°C) for about 35 minutes. Remove weight and bake for a further 10 minutes to slightly brown. Invert onto a serving dish.

This dish can also be made substituting puff pastry for the bread but will not be so traditionally authentic.

Johannes Rosière (1818-1901) *The Fruit Seller*

Soda Bread

This traditional country bread is made without yeast and is a good one to try if you have never made bread before.

Mix 18 fl oz (2 cups) natural yogurt with 2 tablespoons of honey and let the mixture stand awhile. Sift 1 lb (4 cups) whole wheat flour, 1½ teaspoons bicarbonate of soda (baking soda) and 2 teaspoons salt into a large bowl. Rub in 2 tablespoons of butter until the mixture resembles breadcrumbs. Make a well in the centre and pour in the yogurt mixture. Work all the ingredients together until they form a ball. Remove and knead lightly. Form into a flat cake, score a large cross with a knife on the top, sprinkle with sunflower seeds and bake at 375°F (190°C) for an hour or until the bottom sounds hollow when tapped. Buttermilk, if available, could be substituted for yogurt, and could even be said to give a superior taste and texture to the finished bread.

Open thine eyes and thou shalt be satisfied with bread.

Proverbs 20, 13

Camille Pissarro (1830-1903) *Women Haymaking*, 1889

Bread and Butter Pudding

This simple yet heavenly dessert has become so popular that it can regularly be seen on the menus of top class restaurants. It is also a very good way of using up stale bread.

Butter an oblong baking dish and line it with slices of buttered bread cut in half diagonally. Cover with a sprinkling of currants and finely chopped candied lemon and orange peel, another layer of bread, then a few more currants.

Mix together 10 fl oz ($1^{1/4}$ cups) milk and $2^{1/2}$ fl oz ($^{1/4}$ cup) double cream, 2 oz ($^{1/2}$ cup) castor sugar and the grated rind of half a small lemon. Beat up 3 eggs separately then incorporate these into the milk/cream mixture, whisking well. Pour over the bread and sprinkle the top with freshly grated nutmeg. Bake in the oven at 350°F (180°C) for 30-40 minutes and serve warm.

Simplicity is as essential an element in cooking as it is in other arts. Excess in the quantity and variety of spices and condiments is to be especially guarded against.

Charles Francatelli (1805-1876)

Joshua Cristall (1767-1847) *The Gleaners*

Bread Pudding

This is extremely filling but incredibly delicious —
a dish to be made for a special treat when you
feel in need of something comforting to eat.

You can use any kind of left-over bread for
this but remove the crusts and break it up a
bit first. For 4 servings you will need about
8 oz (225 g). Put the bread pieces in a bowl
and pour enough milk over to give it a
good soak but without leaving it too
mushy. Leave soaking for 30 minutes or so
then mix with 2 tablespoons of melted
butter, half a cup of brown sugar,
2 teaspoons of mixed spice and a beaten
egg. Mix well together, then stir in 1 cup
of dried mixed fruit, some candied peel,
some freshly grated nutmeg and the juice of
an orange. Put the mixture in a well
buttered baking dish with some more
brown sugar on top and bake at 350°F
(180°C) for a good hour or so. This is nice
eaten warm but some people like to eat
large slabs of it cold.

Pieter Brueghel the Younger (c.1564–1638) *Harvesters' Lunch*

Green Tomato Chutney

This is a good way, at the end of the season, of using up tomatoes that just will not seem to ripen and is a good standby in the winter larder. A excellent chutney can be made by following this recipe but substituting unripe mangoes instead of the green tomatoes. The British first developed their taste for mango chutney when they were in India and of course it is delicious with curries as well as cold cuts of meat.

Peel and chop 4 lb (2 kg) small green tomatoes, 2 lb (1 kg) cooking apples, 1 lb (450 g) onions and 6 cloves garlic and place them all in a preserving pan. To this add 1 lb (450 g) light brown sugar, 2 tablespoons mustard seed, 1 tablespoon coriander seed, half a teaspoon of celery seed, a teaspoon of turmeric, a tablespoon of salt and $1^{3/4}$ pints (4 cups) white wine vinegar. You could make the chutney even more spicy by adding a few chopped chillies and ginger and cinnamon or cloves. Simmer the mixture for about 2 hours or until it has thickened and reached setting point. Store in covered sterilized jars. This chutney goes well with crusty bread and cheese and a host of other good things.

Italian Bean and Pasta Soup

This is a hearty, 'meal in itself' soup and an excellent source of protein, eminently suitable for vegetarians. It is known as Pasta e Fagioli in Italy where it has been popular for generations. Remember that salt should be added to dried beans towards the end of the cooking process. Salt added too soon will impede the softening process and cause the bean casings to split. A little fat in the cooking water, such as a piece of bacon, salt pork or oil greatly adds to the texture and flavour of the beans but is not absolutely essential.
Another favourite dish, often served as an antipasto and containing cannellini or borlotti beans is Tonno e Fagioli, a delicious concoction of raw red onion rings, flaked tuna and beans laced with a garlicky vinaigrette.

Place 8 oz (1 cup) dried white beans, such as haricots, borlotti or cannellini, into a saucepan, cover with 3 pints (1½ quarts) cold water, boil for 1 minute then turn off the heat and leave to soak for 2 hours. Gently fry a large onion and 2 or 3 cloves of crushed garlic in a little olive oil then add 3 tablespoons tomato purée and a little dried basil. Add to the beans and their soaking water, cover and simmer until tender. Add 4 oz (½ cup) macaroni and boil for a further 10 minutes. Serve with grated Parmesan cheese and some fresh, torn basil. This dish could also be made substituting 2 cans of beans thus avoiding the soaking process.

Gustave Courbet (1819-1877) *The Winnowers*

Jan Victors (1620–1676) *The Fruit Seller*

Apple Sauce

The apple, unlike its more oppulent and luxurious cousin, the pear, does not need to be protected and cossetted to such a degree. The pear needs to be at a crucial stage of ripeness to be enjoyed at its optimum, otherwise it becomes 'sleepy' and virtually inedible.

The apple is far more easy-going. It can be stored for months and is the ultimate convenience food as well as being extremely versatile.

This sauce was traditionally served with rich roasted meats such as pork, goose or duck. It is just as useful, however, in French apple tarts and charlottes, as a first solid food for babies or as a simple dessert with yogurt or cream.

To 1 lb (450 g) cored, peeled and sliced apples you will need 1 tablespoon each of butter, sugar and water and 2 teaspoons of lemon juice. More sugar can be added to taste. Simmer the apples in the water until soft, then beat in the other ingredients.

Tell me what you eat and I will tell you what you are.

Jean Anthelme Brillat-Savarin (1755-1826)

19

Daniel Maclise (1806-1870) *Snapp Apple Night*

Fruit Liqueurs

You hardly need a recipe at all – just one of the following fruits: hulled strawberries, raspberries, blackberries, greengages or other plums, pricked with a needle, dried prunes or apricots which have been soaked in Earl Grey tea, pears, peaches, pineapple, oranges – the list is endless.

Simply pack the fruit in a large glass jar, add a spice such as cloves, a cinnamon stick or a few coriander seeds or crushed cardamom pods. If the fruit is the soft juicy kind add enough castor sugar to come a third of the way up the fruit. For hard fruits, first dissolve 2 cups of sugar to 1 cup water and pour onto the fruit. Top up with gin or vodka, cover and leave in a dark place for a few months or more. To serve, simply strain off the liquid and use the fruit up in desserts or simply eat it as it is.

20

Corn Chowder

This soup is wonderfully comforting and unexpectedly subtle despite its mild ingredients.

Simmer half a cup each of chopped onion, celery, parsley and diced potato in 2 cups of water until half cooked – about 10 minutes. Add 1 cup of fresh raw corn removed from the cob. Simmer with the other vegetables until tender. Add 2 cups of milk and bring up to boiling point without actually boiling. Serve with a knob of butter. Serves 4.

The table is the only place where the first hour is never dull.

Jean Anthelme Brillat-Savarin

Henry Hubert la Thangue (1859-1929) *The Harvester's Supper*

Camille Pissarro (1830-1903) *The Siesta*, 1899

Apple and Blackberry Pie

It really doesn't matter how roughly you drape the pastry over the fruit in the dish – this will only result in a more pleasing rusticity.

Peel, core and slice 6 apples, cover with a little lemon juice and put in a bowl with some vanilla sugar. Empty 4 small punnets of blueberries or blackberries in another bowl and also sprinkle with sugar, (4 oz/^{1}/$_2$ cup in all.) Drape a pie dish with your favourite rich, sweet shortcrust pastry so that there is enough to fold over all round for the top. Pile in the fruits, dot with butter and bring the sides of the pastry over, leaving a small gap in the middle. Brush with egg wash and bake in a hot oven until golden brown.

Cornish Pasties

These pasties are said to have evolved as a sort of packed lunch for the working men of Cornwall to take with them to the fields to eat at midday. In other parts of rural England the pasty was baked with a savoury filling at one end and something like sweetened apple at the other – in other words – a first course and dessert rolled into one!

Roll out 1 lb (450 g) shortcrust pastry and cut into 6 rounds the size of a saucer. Place a mixture of finely chopped raw steak, sliced onions and diced turnips, carrots and potatoes, seasoned with salt and pepper, on one half of each round, moisten the edges with cold water, turn over and firmly seal. Brush with beaten egg and bake in a hot oven for 15 minutes. Reduce the oven to moderate and cook for a further 40 minutes. The pasties can be made using vegetables only and are just as tasty in their own way.

Pickled Walnuts

There is an old adage that wives, dogs and walnut trees benefit greatly from a good beating – not a welcome recommendation in these days of political correctness though I can't speak for the walnut tree! If you are lucky enough to have such a tree in your garden, these pickles are a must. Remember, however, that the walnuts must still be soft and green. After their first flush of youth, walnuts become rather more tough and oily but they are still useful in cakes or pressed into cream cheese. The black North American walnut is somewhat larger than its European cousin and though much harder to crack is more intense in flavour.

Prick about 100 walnuts all over with a fork and cover them in brine made from 4 lb (2 kg) salt and 3 ½ pints (8 cups) water. Soak the walnuts for about 9 days, changing the brine every 3 days. Drain off and place the walnuts on a rack in a warm place or in the sun until they turn black and then pack them into hot sterilized jars. Cover with a mixture of 2 pints (4 cups) vinegar mixed with 1 tablespoon each of peppercorns and chopped ginger and 2 teaspoons of allspice berries which have all been brought to the boil. Seal when cool. They will be ready to eat in a month but will keep for a year or so.

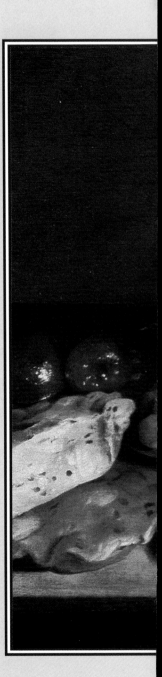

Jacob Foppens van Es (c.1596–1666) *Banquet Still Life*

Bavarian Red Cabbage

The colourful appearance of this dish is good enough reason to make it let alone for its spicy sweetness which goes wonderfully well with pork and bacon dishes.

Remove the damaged outer leaves and coarse ribs from a medium-sized red cabbage. Shred finely and blanch by pouring a kettle of water over it. Leave for 10 minutes and drain well. Put the cabbage into an earthenware casserole together with 2 tablespoons of seedless dried raisins and a cup of diced boiled bacon or gammon, a teaspoon of caraway seeds and 3 tablespoons each of wine vinegar and water. Tightly cover and simmer very gently for about an hour or until cooked but still with a bite to it. Add a teaspoon of sugar and a glass of white wine and cook for a few minutes longer. Thicken the cabbage with a tablespoon of cornflour (cornstarch) or arrowroot mixed with a little water and season well with salt and pepper. Cooking apples make a good substitute for the raisins.

An army marches on its stomach.

Napoléon Bonaparte (1769-1821) who was reputed, amongst other things, to have invented the dish *Chicken Marengo*.

Sauerkraut

This famous dish is widely eaten in Germany and the Alsace region of France where it is known as choucroute and has become part of the way of life there.

Sauerkraut is simply fermented white cabbage produced by layering salt between the shredded leaves. It can be bought commercially prepared but it is still interesting to know how sauerkraut is actually made.

The cabbage, salt and pickle spices are covered and weighted down and left to ferment which it does giving off an unpleasant liquid and ghastly smell in the process. But a wonderful transformation at last takes place, rather like the process of wine-making, and delightful, crunchy sour cabbage is produced to last for a year and be eaten with the famous pork products for which the region is justly famous.

Maud Na

ending the Cabbage Patch

Corn Bread

In the southern states of America corn bread, leavened with baking powder, is served hot with fried chicken or ham or with syrup as a dessert. The tortillas of Central America are made from white cornmeal which has been first soaked in limewater.

Sieve 4 oz ($^2/_3$ cup) cornmeal, 6 oz ($1^1/_2$ cups) plain flour, 2 teaspoons castor sugar, 1 teaspoon each of salt and baking powder together in a bowl. Beat 1 egg and 12 fl oz ($1^1/_2$ cups) milk together and pour them into the flour mixture together with 2 oz (4 tablespoons) melted butter and mix thoroughly. Transfer the mixture to a baking tin and cook in a pre-heated oven at 425°F (220°C) for about 30 minutes. Serve warm or cold, cut into slices and buttered.

The harvest is truly plenteous, but the labourers are few.

Matthew 9, 37

Helene Schjerfbeck (1862-1946) *The Bakery*

Camille Pissarro (1830-1903) *Harvesting at Montfoucault*, 1876

Sweet Potatoes and Apples

This is a variation on the theme of sweet potatoes and yams. Slice the sweet potatoes and place them in a baking dish with alternate layers of sliced apple, scattering raisins and chopped nuts as you go. Sprinkle with lemon juice, a dusting of powdered cinnamon and some dots of butter. Cover and bake in a medium oven for about an hour.

Hot Frothed Beer

This cheerful drink originates from Germany, a country famous for its fine beers, so they must have known a thing or two to have invented such a concoction.

Whisk 4 eggs together very well, strain them, then gradually add 2 pints of ale, whisking all the time. Put the zest and juice of a whole lemon together with half a cup of sugar and half a teaspoon each of powdered ginger, cinnamon and nutmeg into a large saucepan and carefully add the ale and egg mixture. Heat very slowly, whisking all the time. On no account let it boil or it will curdle and be spoiled. Serve the drink hot and very frothy.

Hot Spiced Wine

This is recommended before a bracing autumn or winter walk or even after one and is thought to be a good way of preventing a cold or forgetting one!

Carefully remove the rinds from 6 oranges so that you leave none of the white pith attached. Sprinkle with 8 oz (2 cups) sugar and pour over 3 tablespoons of boiling water. Stir and leave to stand for 40 minutes when the juice will be easy to extract. Place 2 pints good red wine in a large saucepan with 2 bay leaves and heat gently. Stir in the orange rind and syrup then discard the rind and bay leaves and add the orange juice. Stir and continue to heat without actually boiling.

Frans Francken the Elder (c.1542–1616) *A Harvest Feast*

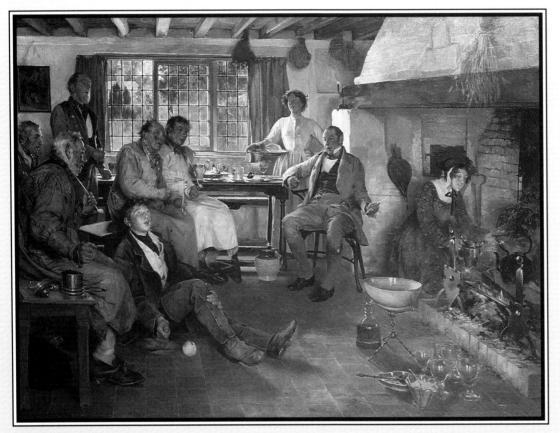

Walter Dendy Sadler (1854–1923) *Preparing the Punch*

Rum Punch

This welcome, cold-weather drink certainly does pack a punch. A farm worker coming in from the chilly work of picking potatoes or tending the sheep would certainly have been looking forward to a glass of two of this. It would be equally acceptable after a cold, windy walk along the cliffs or a day in the garden sweeping up wet leaves.

The punch should be mixed in these proportions and a few cloves or cinnamon sticks could also be added if required. You will need 3 parts of rum, 2 parts of brandy, 6 parts of hot, but not boiling water, 1 part lemon juice and sugar to taste.

The best therapy for all ills is good food.

Léon Daudet (1867-1924)

Fig Conserve

In Italy, the Sicilian fig is the most prized and is eaten with prosciutto or as a dessert. Here is yet another irresistible use for this exotic fruit.

This can be made with 2 lb (1 kg) fresh figs, either green or purple, quartered and put in a pan with the juice and peel of 3 lemons, a cinnamon stick, 3 cloves and 2 lb (4 cups) sugar. Bring slowly to the boil, then boil rapidly until setting point is reached, put into sterilized jars and seal. A more exotic alternative is to use dried figs with 3 tablespoons of pine nuts and 4 oz (1 cup) chopped walnuts added.

Clara Peeters (1594–1659) *The Table*

Sangria

This is a refreshing punch from Spain, ideal to drink on an unexpectedly warm Indian summer day.

For 8-10 people you will need 2 bottles of red wine, the juice of an orange, 2-3 tablespoons of cognac, a thinly sliced lemon, some slices of apple and peach and sugar to taste. Leave for a few hours for the flavours to develop and add soda water, fizzy lemonade and plenty of ice when ready to serve.

Let us eat and drink, for tomorrow we shall die.

Isaiah 17, 13

Vincent van Gogh (1853–1890) *La Méridienne* (after Millet)

Stanhope Alexander Forbes (1857–1947) *The Saffron Cake*

36

Saffron Cake

Saffron is incredibly expensive and no wonder, for each tiny shred is a crocus stigma, of which there are only three to each flower, and these must be carefully gathered by hand and dried. It is most often used as a flavouring and colouring agent in savoury dishes such as paellas, risottos and the rich fish soups and stews of the Mediterranean. Luckily, a very little saffron goes a long way. It should not be confused with turmeric, which is widely used in Indian meat dishes, as the flavour is completely different. Saffron was once widely grown in Cornwall in the south-west of England and is the reason why Saffron Cake became part of the tradition of that region.

Work ¼ oz (½ an envelope dried yeast), a ¼ pint (¾ cup) of warm water and 4 oz (1 cup) flour into a soft dough. Mix well, cover with a cloth and leave in a warm place to rise. Sift another 4 oz flour into a basin with a pinch of salt. Cream together 4 oz (½ cup) butter, 6 oz (1 cup) sugar together with a beaten egg and a packet of saffron, infused in a little warm water, and combine with the yeast dough. Add some seedless raisins and candied peel and knead well into the dough. Put in a greased tin and allow to rise again. Bake in a moderate oven for 1–1½ hours.

Bouillabaisse

This is the famous fish stew of Marseille of which the precious saffron is also a vital ingredient. It depends on rapid boiling during its short cooking period so that the other liquids become emulsified with the olive oil – another important contituent of the dish. For this reason delicate fish are quite inappropriate. Choose instead a mixture of monkfish, gurnard, John Dory, conger eel, haddock, lobster and whiting. It is said that no bouillabaisse is authentic without rascasse. This fish is not easily obtainable outside the Mediterranean but your dish will still taste pretty good without it.

You will need about 3 lb (1½ kg) of assorted fish as suggested above. Clean and scale the fish and cut it into large chunks and place in a large saucepan with 4 cloves of chopped garlic, 3 large chopped tomatoes and 3 finely sliced onions. Add a wine glass of olive oil, a good pinch of saffron, a pinch of thyme, a bay leaf and a sprig each of fresh parsley and fennel. Cover with boiling water, bring back to the boil and boil rapidly for 10 minutes. Separate the fish from the broth and serve this first with fried bread croûtons spread with rouille and grated Gruyère cheese. The fish itself is the second course and you probably won't be able to manage dessert!

English School (18th century) *Dixton Harvesters*

Looks can be deceiving: it's eating that's believing.

James Thurber (1894-1961)

New England Baked Beans

For this recipe you can use dried, cooked beans such as navy, pinto or kidney in just about any combination.

Start by sautéing a chopped onion for a few minutes until tender. Add a grated carrot and a grated apple, tightly cover, and cook very slowly for about five minutes. Mix in 4 cups of the cooked beans, a teaspoon each of salt and mustard powder, half a cup of tomato ketchup and a cup of vegetable stock or water. Cover and bake for 45 minutes.

Mincemeat

It is a good idea to make an early start on this if you are to make your own in sufficient time for it to be well-matured by Christmas.

You will need 1 lb (450 g) cooking (baking) apples, 8 oz (1 generous cup) each of currants, sultanas, mixed candied peel, finely chopped, and shredded beef suet, 12 oz (2 cups) each of raisins and soft brown sugar, the grated rind of 2 oranges and two lemons, 2 tablespoons chopped almonds, 4 teaspoons ground mixed spices, a teaspoon each of ground cinnamon and nutmeg and 6 tablespoons of cognac. Simply mix all the ingredients together, put into sterilized jars, cover with waxed discs, seal and store until ready to use in your tarts and pies.

Daniel Ridgeway Knight (1839-1924) *Gathering Grapes*

Osias Beert the Elder (1570–1624) *Still Life with Bread*

Oatcakes

Oatmeal comes in three grades, coarse, medium and fine. The medium grade is more commonly used to make porridge or to bulk up haggis or sausages. The fine grade is used for making oatcakes and as a coating for herrings before frying — all traditional Scottish dishes. However, the Swiss like it, too, and use it as the main constituent of muesli.

Mix 6 oz (1 cup) oatmeal with a pinch of bicarbonate of soda and a pinch of salt. Melt 2 tablespoons of dripping or bacon fat and mix with a tablespoon of water. Add the oatmeal and mix to the consistency of firm pastry, adding boiling water as necessary. Roll out thinly and cut into rounds with a pastry cutter. Place on a floured baking tray and bake in a moderate oven until brown and crisp. Serve with kippers for breakfast or with butter and marmalade or goat's cheese.

Bread Sauce

This is usually served with poultry and despite its prosaic name is actually delicious.

Stud a medium-sized onion with dried cloves and place with 6 black peppercorns and a bay leaf in a saucepan containing 15 fl oz (2 cups) milk. Add a little salt and bring the whole lot to the boil. Remove from the heat, cover and allow to infuse for a couple of hours. When you are ready to continue with the sauce, remove the peppercorns and bay leaf and remove but reserve the onion. Stir in 3 oz (1 cup) freshly made breadcrumbs and a good knob of butter. Leave on a mere glimmer of heat until the breadcrumbs swell and thicken the sauce. Replace the onion and leave in a warm place until needed. Remove onion and add a few tablespoons of cream before serving.

William Frederick Yeames (1835-1918) *Cherry Ripe*

Cherry Tart

Fruit tarts are one of France's traditional desserts and you will find them on the menu of every restaurant. They can also be bought from any local pâtisserie to finish off a home-cooked meal.

For this dish the dark, slightly sharp morello cherry is best and you should start by pitting and gently cooking about 1½ lb (1½ quarts) with 2 oz (4 tablespoons) unsalted butter, 3 oz (½ cup) sugar and 3 tablespoons of Calvados for about 7 minutes until the cherries are tender and slightly caramelized. Remove the cherries with a slotted spoon. Put the remaining cooled juice into a bowl and pour in ¼ pint (¾ cup) of double cream and whisk until firm. Fold in 8 oz (1 cup) fromage frais. Spread this mixture over a case of puff pastry, which you have baked blind, and arrange the cherries on top.

Angelo Martinetti (19th century) *Reciting an Ode on Mamma's Birthday*

Caraway Cake

People either loathe or love this seedy cake but it is still a well remembered part of childhood.

Cream 8 oz (1 cup) butter with 5 oz ($\frac{1}{2}$ cup) sugar until smooth and pale. Sieve 5 oz (1 cup) self-raising flour and 4 tablespoons cornflour (cornstarch) together with a pinch of salt. Add one egg and half the flour to the butter and sugar mixture, beating it well in. Then add another egg and the rest of the flour. Finally, stir in 2 tablespoons of milk and enough dried caraway seeds to lightly speckle the mixture. Turn into a buttered and floured cake tin and bake at 350°F (180°C) for a good 1$\frac{1}{4}$ hours. Test with a skewer after an hour's cooking.

Camille Pissarro (1830-1903) *Apple Pickers, Eragny*, 1888

44

Omelette aux Pommes

Savoury omelettes filled with all manner of things, from vegetables and cheese to ham and smoked haddock, as in Omelette Arnold Bennett, are justifiably popular as a light and nourishing lunch or supper dish. Sweet omelettes are less common but popular in France and would make a good dessert after a light first course. You could, of course, use other fruits such as pears or apricots and vary the kinds of liqueurs used – cognac, Calvados or kirsch, for example.

Peel and slice 2 tart, crisp eating apples and leave to macerate for half an hour or so in 4 tablespoons of dark rum. Remove apples from the marinade and cook them in a little butter until tender. In a bowl, whisk together 5 egg yolks, the rum mixture and a little sugar until frothy. Whisk up the egg whites and gently fold into the yolks. Halve the mixture, melt some butter and make two omelettes, cooking them briefly on both sides and using a plate to help you turn them. Fill with the apple mixture and serve immediately.

My definition of Man is, a 'Cooking Animal'. The beasts have memory, judgement, and all the facilities and passions of our mind ... but no beast is a cook.

Samuel Johnson (1709-1784)

Winslow Homer (1836-1910) *The Veteran in a New Field*

Pickled Onions

These are an integral part of the British Ploughman's Lunch, of possibly mythical origins, now mostly eaten as a pub lunch but thought to be what the agricultural worker in days of yore would have taken with him to the fields for his midday meal. This would have consisted of a crusty farmhouse loaf, some tasty cheese and, of course, some pickled onions! Nevertheless, they continue to be extremely popular and won't hang around for too long — so it is wise to make plenty.

Put 4lb (2 kg) small pickling onions in a bowl and cover them with boiling water. This will make them easier to peel. Put the onions back in the drained bowl, sprinkle with 1 cup of coarse sea salt and leave covered with water for about 24 hours. Drain and rinse. Meanwhile, put 5 cups of white vinegar, a little chopped ginger, 6 chillies, 6 cloves, 2 teaspoons mustard seeds and a tablespoon of black peppercorns into a saucepan, bring to the boil, cook for 5 minutes, remove from the heat and allow to cool. Pack the onions in sterilized jars, cover with the vinegar mixture and seal.

Imperial/Metric Conversion

Weights

2 oz	50 g
2½ oz	60 g
3 oz	75 g
4 oz	110 g
4½ oz	125 g
5 oz	150 g
6 oz	175 g
7 oz	200 g
8 oz	225 g
9 oz	250 g
10 oz	275 g
12 oz	350 g
1 lb	450 g
1½ lb	700 g
2 lb	900 g
3 lb	1.3 kg

Volume

5 fl oz (¼ pt)	150 ml
10 fl oz (½ pt)	275 ml
15 fl oz (¾ pt)	425 ml
1 pint	570 ml
1¼ pints	725 ml
1¾ pints	1 litre
2 pints	1.2 litres
2½ pints	1.5 litres
4 pints	2.25 litres

Index

C.H. Hart (19th century) *The Harvest*